THE BUSY COOK'S

Recipe Reminder

Your personal index
to favorite
cookbook recipes

Published in the United States by HollyDay Books

Printed at Bolger Publications/Creative Printing, Minneapolis
Technical advisors: Jane Eschweiler, Julia Odell, Jack Bolger

Inquiries and orders can be addressed to:

HollyDay Books
130 Ashley Road
Hopkins, Minnesota 55343

another great idea from HollyDay Books
ISBN-0-943786-02-9

Tired of leafing through page after page, cookbook after cookbook, searching for that favorite recipe? Then this is the book for you! In a simple format that takes only seconds to do, you can now index all those favorites, making them easily accessible and saving you valuable time. An added feature is an entertainment section to record whom you entertained, what you served, and which cookbooks you used. You spend so much time in the kitchen, why not make things a little easier for yourself. This handy little book will help.

Happy cooking!

How This Book Works

Recipes fall into many different categories. Some are quick and easy, others more difficult, there are family favorites, dishes that children especially like and special ones for company. The problem is that if you have more than one cookbook, which most cooks do, it can be nearly impossible to remember which recipe is where. Now you can log those recipes which you especially want to keep track of. The format is simple: Suppose you have baked a chocolate cake which the entire family thought was wonderful, the best. You will probably want to bake it again sometime, right? So then turn to the section "Cakes, Cookies and Pies" and write:

. . . .
RECIPE   COOKBOOK   PAGE

Chocolate Cake   Joy of Cooking   627

COMMENTS
delicious, moist. Everyone loved it.
. . . .

Six months from now when someone asks why you haven't baked that great chocolate cake again you can find it right away by turning to the Recipe Reminder instead of going through ten cookbooks searching for it.

This Reminder is not meant to index every recipe you ever cook, but just the ones you want to keep track of. Take the time to log them in and at least one small corner of your life might be a little less complicated.

Index

Appetizers

RECIPE   COOKBOOK   PAGE

COMMENTS

. . . .
RECIPE   COOKBOOK   PAGE

COMMENTS

. . . .
RECIPE   COOKBOOK   PAGE

COMMENTS

RECIPE   COOKBOOK   PAGE

COMMENTS

. . . .

RECIPE   COOKBOOK   PAGE

COMMENTS

. . . .

RECIPE   COOKBOOK   PAGE

COMMENTS

. . . .

RECIPE   COOKBOOK   PAGE

COMMENTS

. . . .

RECIPE   COOKBOOK   PAGE

COMMENTS

. . . .

RECIPE   COOKBOOK   PAGE

COMMENTS

RECIPE   COOKBOOK   PAGE

COMMENTS

. . . .
RECIPE   COOKBOOK   PAGE

COMMENTS

. . . .
RECIPE   COOKBOOK   PAGE

COMMENTS

. . . .
RECIPE   COOKBOOK   PAGE

COMMENTS

. . . .
RECIPE   COOKBOOK   PAGE

COMMENTS

. . . .
RECIPE   COOKBOOK   PAGE

COMMENTS

RECIPE   COOKBOOK   PAGE

COMMENTS

RECIPE   COOKBOOK   PAGE

COMMENTS

RECIPE   COOKBOOK   PAGE

COMMENTS

RECIPE   COOKBOOK   PAGE

COMMENTS

RECIPE   COOKBOOK   PAGE

COMMENTS

RECIPE   COOKBOOK   PAGE

COMMENTS

Beverages

RECIPE   COOKBOOK   PAGE

COMMENTS

. . . .

RECIPE   COOKBOOK   PAGE

COMMENTS

. . . .

RECIPE   COOKBOOK   PAGE

COMMENTS

RECIPE   COOKBOOK   PAGE

COMMENTS

. . . .

RECIPE   COOKBOOK   PAGE

COMMENTS

. . . .

RECIPE   COOKBOOK   PAGE

COMMENTS

. . . .

RECIPE   COOKBOOK   PAGE

COMMENTS

. . . .

RECIPE   COOKBOOK   PAGE

COMMENTS

. . . .

RECIPE   COOKBOOK   PAGE

COMMENTS

RECIPE   COOKBOOK   PAGE

COMMENTS

. . . .
RECIPE   COOKBOOK   PAGE

COMMENTS

. . . .
RECIPE   COOKBOOK   PAGE

COMMENTS

. . . .
RECIPE   COOKBOOK   PAGE

COMMENTS

. . . .
RECIPE   COOKBOOK   PAGE

COMMENTS

. . . .
RECIPE   COOKBOOK   PAGE

COMMENTS

RECIPE   COOKBOOK   PAGE

COMMENTS

RECIPE   COOKBOOK   PAGE

COMMENTS

RECIPE   COOKBOOK   PAGE

COMMENTS

RECIPE   COOKBOOK   PAGE

COMMENTS

RECIPE   COOKBOOK   PAGE

COMMENTS

RECIPE   COOKBOOK   PAGE

COMMENTS

Meats

RECIPE	COOKBOOK	PAGE
BBQ Spareribs	Crockery Cookery large, soft cover	p. 76

COMMENTS

Sauce, same page

. . . .

RECIPE	COOKBOOK BH & G	PAGE
Pork Chops w Mushroom Sauce	New Crockery Cooker Cook Book - large, hard - cover	26

COMMENTS

Shawn + Pap + I liked them!

. . . .

RECIPE	COOKBOOK	PAGE
Pork Chops & Potatoes	The I Hate To Cook Book	20

COMMENTS

Easy for a busy day - good, too.

RECIPE   COOKBOOK   PAGE

COMMENTS

. . . .
RECIPE   COOKBOOK   PAGE

COMMENTS

. . . .
RECIPE   COOKBOOK   PAGE

COMMENTS

. . . .
RECIPE   COOKBOOK   PAGE

COMMENTS

. . . .
RECIPE   COOKBOOK   PAGE

COMMENTS

. . . .
RECIPE   COOKBOOK   PAGE

COMMENTS

RECIPE   COOKBOOK   PAGE

COMMENTS

. . . .
RECIPE   COOKBOOK   PAGE

COMMENTS

. . . .
RECIPE   COOKBOOK   PAGE

COMMENTS

. . . .
RECIPE   COOKBOOK   PAGE

COMMENTS

. . . .
RECIPE   COOKBOOK   PAGE

COMMENTS

. . . .
RECIPE   COOKBOOK   PAGE

COMMENTS

RECIPE   COOKBOOK   PAGE

COMMENTS

RECIPE   COOKBOOK   PAGE

COMMENTS

RECIPE   COOKBOOK   PAGE

COMMENTS

RECIPE   COOKBOOK   PAGE

COMMENTS

RECIPE   COOKBOOK   PAGE

COMMENTS

RECIPE   COOKBOOK   PAGE

COMMENTS

Poultry

RECIPE   COOKBOOK   PAGE

COMMENTS

. . . .

RECIPE   COOKBOOK   PAGE

COMMENTS

. . . .

RECIPE   COOKBOOK   PAGE

COMMENTS

RECIPE   COOKBOOK   PAGE

COMMENTS

. . . .
RECIPE   COOKBOOK   PAGE

COMMENTS

. . . .
RECIPE   COOKBOOK   PAGE

COMMENTS

. . . .
RECIPE   COOKBOOK   PAGE

COMMENTS

. . . .
RECIPE   COOKBOOK   PAGE

COMMENTS

. . . .
RECIPE   COOKBOOK   PAGE

COMMENTS

RECIPE   COOKBOOK   PAGE

COMMENTS

. . . .
RECIPE   COOKBOOK   PAGE

COMMENTS

. . . .
RECIPE   COOKBOOK   PAGE

COMMENTS

. . . .
RECIPE   COOKBOOK   PAGE

COMMENTS

. . . .
RECIPE   COOKBOOK   PAGE

COMMENTS

. . . .
RECIPE   COOKBOOK   PAGE

COMMENTS

RECIPE   COOKBOOK   PAGE

COMMENTS

. . . .

RECIPE   COOKBOOK   PAGE

COMMENTS

. . . .

RECIPE   COOKBOOK   PAGE

COMMENTS

. . . .

RECIPE   COOKBOOK   PAGE

COMMENTS

. . . .

RECIPE   COOKBOOK   PAGE

COMMENTS

. . . .

RECIPE   COOKBOOK   PAGE

COMMENTS

Fish, Shellfish

RECIPE	COOKBOOK	PAGE
Tuna Macaroni Casserole	*BH & G All-time Favorite Casserole Recipes*	*20*

COMMENTS

Dick liked it (said so, twice) — I did, too,

. . . .

RECIPE	COOKBOOK	PAGE

COMMENTS

. . . .

RECIPE	COOKBOOK	PAGE

COMMENTS

RECIPE   COOKBOOK   PAGE

COMMENTS

RECIPE   COOKBOOK   PAGE

COMMENTS

RECIPE   COOKBOOK   PAGE

COMMENTS

RECIPE   COOKBOOK   PAGE

COMMENTS

RECIPE   COOKBOOK   PAGE

COMMENTS

RECIPE   COOKBOOK   PAGE

COMMENTS

RECIPE   COOKBOOK   PAGE

COMMENTS

. . . .
RECIPE   COOKBOOK   PAGE

COMMENTS

. . . .
RECIPE   COOKBOOK   PAGE

COMMENTS

. . . .
RECIPE   COOKBOOK   PAGE

COMMENTS

. . . .
RECIPE   COOKBOOK   PAGE

COMMENTS

. . . .
RECIPE   COOKBOOK   PAGE

COMMENTS

RECIPE   COOKBOOK   PAGE

COMMENTS

. . . .

RECIPE   COOKBOOK   PAGE

COMMENTS

. . . .

RECIPE   COOKBOOK   PAGE

COMMENTS

. . . .

RECIPE   COOKBOOK   PAGE

COMMENTS

. . . .

RECIPE   COOKBOOK   PAGE

COMMENTS

. . . .

RECIPE   COOKBOOK   PAGE

COMMENTS

Casseroles

RECIPE   COOKBOOK   PAGE

COMMENTS

. . . .
RECIPE   COOKBOOK   PAGE

COMMENTS

. . . .
RECIPE   COOKBOOK   PAGE

COMMENTS

RECIPE   COOKBOOK   PAGE

COMMENTS

. . . .
RECIPE   COOKBOOK   PAGE

COMMENTS

. . . .
RECIPE   COOKBOOK   PAGE

COMMENTS

. . . .
RECIPE   COOKBOOK   PAGE

COMMENTS

. . . .
RECIPE   COOKBOOK   PAGE

COMMENTS

. . . .
RECIPE   COOKBOOK   PAGE

COMMENTS

RECIPE   COOKBOOK   PAGE

COMMENTS

. . . .
RECIPE   COOKBOOK   PAGE

COMMENTS

. . . .
RECIPE   COOKBOOK   PAGE

COMMENTS

. . . .
RECIPE   COOKBOOK   PAGE

COMMENTS

. . . .
RECIPE   COOKBOOK   PAGE

COMMENTS

. . . .
RECIPE   COOKBOOK   PAGE

COMMENTS

RECIPE   COOKBOOK   PAGE

COMMENTS

RECIPE   COOKBOOK   PAGE

COMMENTS

RECIPE   COOKBOOK   PAGE

COMMENTS

RECIPE   COOKBOOK   PAGE

COMMENTS

RECIPE   COOKBOOK   PAGE

COMMENTS

RECIPE   COOKBOOK   PAGE

COMMENTS

Eggs and Cheese

RECIPE   COOKBOOK   PAGE

COMMENTS

. . . .

RECIPE   COOKBOOK   PAGE

COMMENTS

. . . .

RECIPE   COOKBOOK   PAGE

COMMENTS

RECIPE   COOKBOOK   PAGE

COMMENTS

. . . .
RECIPE   COOKBOOK   PAGE

COMMENTS

. . . .
RECIPE   COOKBOOK   PAGE

COMMENTS

. . . .
RECIPE   COOKBOOK   PAGE

COMMENTS

. . . .
RECIPE   COOKBOOK   PAGE

COMMENTS

. . . .
RECIPE   COOKBOOK   PAGE

COMMENTS

RECIPE   COOKBOOK   PAGE

COMMENTS

. . . .
RECIPE   COOKBOOK   PAGE

COMMENTS

. . . .
RECIPE   COOKBOOK   PAGE

COMMENTS

. . . .
RECIPE   COOKBOOK   PAGE

COMMENTS

. . . .
RECIPE   COOKBOOK   PAGE

COMMENTS

. . . .
RECIPE   COOKBOOK   PAGE

COMMENTS

RECIPE   COOKBOOK   PAGE

COMMENTS

RECIPE   COOKBOOK   PAGE

COMMENTS

RECIPE   COOKBOOK   PAGE

COMMENTS

RECIPE   COOKBOOK   PAGE

COMMENTS

RECIPE   COOKBOOK   PAGE

COMMENTS

RECIPE   COOKBOOK   PAGE

COMMENTS

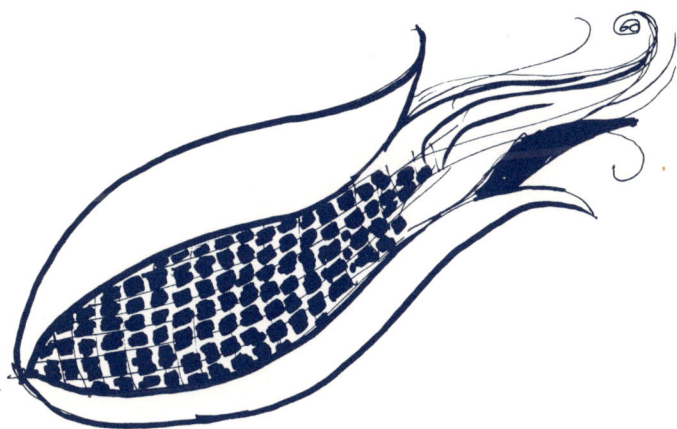

Vegetables

RECIPE   COOKBOOK   PAGE

Easy Baked Beans   BH & G   300

COMMENTS   Good! (with bacon on top)

. . . .

RECIPE   COOKBOOK   PAGE

Parsleyed Carrots   The Everything Cookbook
(basic recipe)   (from mom)   530 - 531

COMMENTS

         Good!

. . . .

RECIPE   COOKBOOK   PAGE

Zucchini Casserole   The Everything Cookbook
                    (from mom)   558
                                                    (557)

COMMENTS

Love it!

(oven)

RECIPE
Stuffed Peppers
(Beef in Pepper Cups)

COOKBOOK
BH&G all-time
Favorite Vegetable
Recipes

PAGE
69

COMMENTS

. . . .

RECIPE COOKBOOK PAGE

COMMENTS

. . . .

RECIPE COOKBOOK PAGE

COMMENTS

. . . .

RECIPE COOKBOOK PAGE

COMMENTS

. . . .

RECIPE COOKBOOK PAGE

COMMENTS

. . . .

RECIPE COOKBOOK PAGE

COMMENTS

RECIPE   COOKBOOK   PAGE

COMMENTS

. . . .
RECIPE   COOKBOOK   PAGE

COMMENTS

. . . .
RECIPE   COOKBOOK   PAGE

COMMENTS

. . . .
RECIPE   COOKBOOK   PAGE

COMMENTS

. . . .
RECIPE   COOKBOOK   PAGE

COMMENTS

. . . .
RECIPE   COOKBOOK   PAGE

COMMENTS

RECIPE   COOKBOOK   PAGE

COMMENTS

. . . .
RECIPE   COOKBOOK   PAGE

COMMENTS

. . . .
RECIPE   COOKBOOK   PAGE

COMMENTS

. . . .
RECIPE   COOKBOOK   PAGE

COMMENTS

. . . .
RECIPE   COOKBOOK   PAGE

COMMENTS

. . . .
RECIPE   COOKBOOK   PAGE

COMMENTS

Soups and
Sandwiches

RECIPE   COOKBOOK   PAGE

COMMENTS

. . . .
RECIPE   COOKBOOK   PAGE

COMMENTS

. . . .
RECIPE   COOKBOOK   PAGE

COMMENTS

RECIPE   COOKBOOK   PAGE

COMMENTS

RECIPE   COOKBOOK   PAGE

COMMENTS

RECIPE   COOKBOOK   PAGE

COMMENTS

RECIPE   COOKBOOK   PAGE

COMMENTS

RECIPE   COOKBOOK   PAGE

COMMENTS

RECIPE   COOKBOOK   PAGE

COMMENTS

RECIPE   COOKBOOK   PAGE

COMMENTS

. . . .
RECIPE   COOKBOOK   PAGE

COMMENTS

. . . .
RECIPE   COOKBOOK   PAGE

COMMENTS

. . . .
RECIPE   COOKBOOK   PAGE

COMMENTS

. . . .
RECIPE   COOKBOOK   PAGE

COMMENTS

. . . .
RECIPE   COOKBOOK   PAGE

COMMENTS

RECIPE   COOKBOOK   PAGE

COMMENTS

RECIPE   COOKBOOK   PAGE

COMMENTS

RECIPE   COOKBOOK   PAGE

COMMENTS

RECIPE   COOKBOOK   PAGE

COMMENTS

RECIPE   COOKBOOK   PAGE

COMMENTS

RECIPE   COOKBOOK   PAGE

COMMENTS

Pasta

RECIPE   COOKBOOK   PAGE

COMMENTS

. . . .
RECIPE   COOKBOOK   PAGE

COMMENTS

. . . .
RECIPE   COOKBOOK   PAGE

COMMENTS

RECIPE   COOKBOOK   PAGE

COMMENTS

. . . .

RECIPE   COOKBOOK   PAGE

COMMENTS

. . . .

RECIPE   COOKBOOK   PAGE

COMMENTS

. . . .

RECIPE   COOKBOOK   PAGE

COMMENTS

. . . .

RECIPE   COOKBOOK   PAGE

COMMENTS

. . . .

RECIPE   COOKBOOK   PAGE

COMMENTS

RECIPE   COOKBOOK   PAGE

COMMENTS

. . . .
RECIPE   COOKBOOK   PAGE

COMMENTS

. . . .
RECIPE   COOKBOOK   PAGE

COMMENTS

. . . .
RECIPE   COOKBOOK   PAGE

COMMENTS

. . . .
RECIPE   COOKBOOK   PAGE

COMMENTS

. . . .
RECIPE   COOKBOOK   PAGE

COMMENTS

RECIPE   COOKBOOK   PAGE

COMMENTS

. . . .

RECIPE   COOKBOOK   PAGE

COMMENTS

. . . .

RECIPE   COOKBOOK   PAGE

COMMENTS

. . . .

RECIPE   COOKBOOK   PAGE

COMMENTS

. . . .

RECIPE   COOKBOOK   PAGE

COMMENTS

. . . .

RECIPE   COOKBOOK   PAGE

COMMENTS

Salads

RECIPE   COOKBOOK   PAGE

COMMENTS

. . . .

RECIPE   COOKBOOK   PAGE

COMMENTS

. . . .

RECIPE   COOKBOOK   PAGE

COMMENTS

RECIPE   COOKBOOK   PAGE

COMMENTS

. . . .
RECIPE   COOKBOOK   PAGE

COMMENTS

. . . .
RECIPE   COOKBOOK   PAGE

COMMENTS

. . . .
RECIPE   COOKBOOK   PAGE

COMMENTS

. . . .
RECIPE   COOKBOOK   PAGE

COMMENTS

. . . .
RECIPE   COOKBOOK   PAGE

COMMENTS

RECIPE   COOKBOOK   PAGE

COMMENTS

. . . .
RECIPE   COOKBOOK   PAGE

COMMENTS

. . . .
RECIPE   COOKBOOK   PAGE

COMMENTS

. . . .
RECIPE   COOKBOOK   PAGE

COMMENTS

. . . .
RECIPE   COOKBOOK   PAGE

COMMENTS

. . . .
RECIPE   COOKBOOK   PAGE

COMMENTS

RECIPE   COOKBOOK   PAGE

COMMENTS

. . . .
RECIPE   COOKBOOK   PAGE

COMMENTS

. . . .
RECIPE   COOKBOOK   PAGE

COMMENTS

. . . .
RECIPE   COOKBOOK   PAGE

COMMENTS

. . . .
RECIPE   COOKBOOK   PAGE

COMMENTS

. . . .
RECIPE   COOKBOOK   PAGE

COMMENTS

Breads

RECIPE   COOKBOOK   PAGE

COMMENTS

. . . .
RECIPE   COOKBOOK   PAGE

COMMENTS

. . . .
RECIPE   COOKBOOK   PAGE

COMMENTS

RECIPE   COOKBOOK   PAGE

COMMENTS

RECIPE   COOKBOOK   PAGE

COMMENTS

RECIPE   COOKBOOK   PAGE

COMMENTS

RECIPE   COOKBOOK   PAGE

COMMENTS

RECIPE   COOKBOOK   PAGE

COMMENTS

RECIPE   COOKBOOK   PAGE

COMMENTS

RECIPE   COOKBOOK   PAGE

COMMENTS

. . . .

RECIPE   COOKBOOK   PAGE

COMMENTS

. . . .

RECIPE   COOKBOOK   PAGE

COMMENTS

. . . .

RECIPE   COOKBOOK   PAGE

COMMENTS

. . . .

RECIPE   COOKBOOK   PAGE

COMMENTS

. . . .

RECIPE   COOKBOOK   PAGE

COMMENTS

RECIPE   COOKBOOK   PAGE

COMMENTS

. . . .
RECIPE   COOKBOOK   PAGE

COMMENTS

. . . .
RECIPE   COOKBOOK   PAGE

COMMENTS

. . . .
RECIPE   COOKBOOK   PAGE

COMMENTS

. . . .
RECIPE   COOKBOOK   PAGE

COMMENTS

. . . .
RECIPE   COOKBOOK   PAGE

COMMENTS

Cakes,
Cookies and Pies

RECIPE   COOKBOOK   PAGE

COMMENTS

. . . .

RECIPE   COOKBOOK   PAGE

COMMENTS

. . . .

RECIPE   COOKBOOK   PAGE

COMMENTS

RECIPE   COOKBOOK   PAGE

COMMENTS

RECIPE   COOKBOOK   PAGE

COMMENTS

RECIPE   COOKBOOK   PAGE

COMMENTS

RECIPE   COOKBOOK   PAGE

COMMENTS

RECIPE   COOKBOOK   PAGE

COMMENTS

RECIPE   COOKBOOK   PAGE

COMMENTS

RECIPE   COOKBOOK   PAGE

COMMENTS

. . . .

RECIPE   COOKBOOK   PAGE

COMMENTS

. . . .

RECIPE   COOKBOOK   PAGE

COMMENTS

. . . .

RECIPE   COOKBOOK   PAGE

COMMENTS

. . . .

RECIPE   COOKBOOK   PAGE

COMMENTS

. . . .

RECIPE   COOKBOOK   PAGE

COMMENTS

RECIPE   COOKBOOK   PAGE

COMMENTS

. . . .
RECIPE   COOKBOOK   PAGE

COMMENTS

. . . .
RECIPE   COOKBOOK   PAGE

COMMENTS

. . . .
RECIPE   COOKBOOK   PAGE

COMMENTS

. . . .
RECIPE   COOKBOOK   PAGE

COMMENTS

. . . .
RECIPE   COOKBOOK   PAGE

COMMENTS

Other Desserts

RECIPE   COOKBOOK   PAGE

COMMENTS

· ·
RECIPE   COOKBOOK   PAGE

COMMENTS

· ·
RECIPE   COOKBOOK   PAGE

COMMENTS

RECIPE   COOKBOOK   PAGE

COMMENTS

. . . .

RECIPE   COOKBOOK   PAGE

COMMENTS

. . . .

RECIPE   COOKBOOK   PAGE

COMMENTS

. . . .

RECIPE   COOKBOOK   PAGE

COMMENTS

. . . .

RECIPE   COOKBOOK   PAGE

COMMENTS

. . . .

RECIPE   COOKBOOK   PAGE

COMMENTS

RECIPE   COOKBOOK   PAGE

COMMENTS

. . . .
RECIPE   COOKBOOK   PAGE

COMMENTS

. . . .
RECIPE   COOKBOOK   PAGE

COMMENTS

. . . .
RECIPE   COOKBOOK   PAGE

COMMENTS

. . . .
RECIPE   COOKBOOK   PAGE

COMMENTS

. . . .
RECIPE   COOKBOOK   PAGE

COMMENTS

RECIPE   COOKBOOK   PAGE

COMMENTS

. . . .
RECIPE   COOKBOOK   PAGE

COMMENTS

. . . .
RECIPE   COOKBOOK   PAGE

COMMENTS

. . . .
RECIPE   COOKBOOK   PAGE

COMMENTS

. . . .
RECIPE   COOKBOOK   PAGE

COMMENTS

. . . .
RECIPE   COOKBOOK   PAGE

COMMENTS

Ethnic Foods

RECIPE   COOKBOOK   PAGE

Chili   BH&G Crockery Cookbook   *35*

(hard-cover)

COMMENTS

good — makes double batch

. . . .

RECIPE   COOKBOOK   PAGE

COMMENTS

. . . .

RECIPE   COOKBOOK   PAGE

COMMENTS

RECIPE   COOKBOOK   PAGE

COMMENTS

. . . .

RECIPE   COOKBOOK   PAGE

COMMENTS

. . . .

RECIPE   COOKBOOK   PAGE

COMMENTS

. . . .

RECIPE   COOKBOOK   PAGE

COMMENTS

. . . .

RECIPE   COOKBOOK   PAGE

COMMENTS

. . . .

RECIPE   COOKBOOK   PAGE

COMMENTS

RECIPE   COOKBOOK   PAGE

COMMENTS

. . . .
RECIPE   COOKBOOK   PAGE

COMMENTS

. . . .
RECIPE   COOKBOOK   PAGE

COMMENTS

. . . .
RECIPE   COOKBOOK   PAGE

COMMENTS

. . . .
RECIPE   COOKBOOK   PAGE

COMMENTS

. . . .
RECIPE   COOKBOOK   PAGE

COMMENTS

RECIPE   COOKBOOK   PAGE

COMMENTS

. . . .
RECIPE   COOKBOOK   PAGE

COMMENTS

. . . .
RECIPE   COOKBOOK   PAGE

COMMENTS

. . . .
RECIPE   COOKBOOK   PAGE

COMMENTS

. . . .
RECIPE   COOKBOOK   PAGE

COMMENTS

. . . .
RECIPE   COOKBOOK   PAGE

COMMENTS

Holiday Cooking

RECIPE   COOKBOOK   PAGE

COMMENTS

. . . .

RECIPE   COOKBOOK   PAGE

COMMENTS

. . . .

RECIPE   COOKBOOK   PAGE

COMMENTS

RECIPE   COOKBOOK   PAGE

COMMENTS

. . . .
RECIPE   COOKBOOK   PAGE

COMMENTS

. . . .
RECIPE   COOKBOOK   PAGE

COMMENTS

. . . .
RECIPE   COOKBOOK   PAGE

COMMENTS

. . . .
RECIPE   COOKBOOK   PAGE

COMMENTS

. . . .
RECIPE   COOKBOOK   PAGE

COMMENTS

RECIPE   COOKBOOK   PAGE

COMMENTS

. . . .

RECIPE   COOKBOOK   PAGE

COMMENTS

. . . .

RECIPE   COOKBOOK   PAGE

COMMENTS

. . . .

RECIPE   COOKBOOK   PAGE

COMMENTS

. . . .

RECIPE   COOKBOOK   PAGE

COMMENTS

. . . .

RECIPE   COOKBOOK   PAGE

COMMENTS

RECIPE   COOKBOOK   PAGE

COMMENTS

. . . .

RECIPE   COOKBOOK   PAGE

COMMENTS

. . . .

RECIPE   COOKBOOK   PAGE

COMMENTS

. . . .

RECIPE   COOKBOOK   PAGE

COMMENTS

. . . .

RECIPE   COOKBOOK   PAGE

COMMENTS

. . . .

RECIPE   COOKBOOK   PAGE

COMMENTS

Children's Favorites

RECIPE   COOKBOOK   PAGE

COMMENTS

. . . .

RECIPE   COOKBOOK   PAGE

COMMENTS

. . . .

RECIPE   COOKBOOK   PAGE

COMMENTS

RECIPE   COOKBOOK   PAGE

COMMENTS

. . . .
RECIPE   COOKBOOK   PAGE

COMMENTS

. . . .
RECIPE   COOKBOOK   PAGE

COMMENTS

. . . .
RECIPE   COOKBOOK   PAGE

COMMENTS

. . . .
RECIPE   COOKBOOK   PAGE

COMMENTS

. . . .
RECIPE   COOKBOOK   PAGE

COMMENTS

DATE
GUESTS

MENU   COOKBOOKS   PAGE

COMMENTS

. . . .

DATE
GUESTS

MENU   COOKBOOKS   PAGE

COMMENTS

DATE
GUESTS

MENU   COOKBOOKS   PAGE

COMMENTS

DATE
GUESTS

MENU   COOKBOOKS   PAGE

COMMENTS

Entertaining

Who ate what and when

DATE
GUESTS

MENU   COOKBOOKS   PAGE

COMMENTS

DATE
GUESTS

MENU   COOKBOOKS   PAGE

COMMENTS

. . . .
DATE
GUESTS

MENU   COOKBOOKS   PAGE

COMMENTS

DATE
GUESTS

MENU   COOKBOOKS   PAGE

COMMENTS

. . . .

DATE
GUESTS

MENU   COOKBOOKS   PAGE

COMMENTS

DATE
GUESTS

MENU   COOKBOOKS   PAGE

COMMENTS

· ·
DATE
GUESTS

MENU   COOKBOOKS   PAGE

COMMENTS

Recipe Reminder

Easy Order Form

Please send me _____ copies of the Busy Cook's Recipe Reminder at $6.50 each (includes postage and handling).

TOTAL ENCLOSED $_____

_____
NAME

_____
ADDRESS

_____
CITY/STATE/ZIP

Make checks payable to: HollyDay Books, 130 Ashley Rd., Hopkins, MN 55343

Recipe Reminder

Easy Order Form

Please send me _____ copies of the Busy Cook's Recipe Reminder at $6.50 each (includes postage and handling).

TOTAL ENCLOSED $_____

_____
NAME

_____
ADDRESS

_____
CITY/STATE/ZIP

Make checks payable to: HollyDay Books, 130 Ashley Rd., Hopkins, MN 55343